Giovanna Magi

BANGKOK
AYUTTHAYA · PATTAYA

Printed in Italy by Centro Stampa Editoriale Bonechi
Photographs from the Archives of Casa Editrice Bonechi

Translated by Susan Fraser

ISBN 88-7009-475-8

* * *

GLOSSARY

We report here below, in alfabetical order, a concise glossary of the usual thai words which signify artistic and architectural elements.

Bot
It is the most sacred part of the building, where monks were ordained. It generally consists of a single lengthened nave, sometimes divided into several naves by two rows of columns. The walls can be opened by one or more windows; several doors open onto the entrance façade, whose central façade is larger than the other ones.

Chedi
Of Ceylonese inspiration, this building comes from the Indian stupa; it consists of a base and a bell-shaped dome crowned by a cubic reliquary that terminates in a point. It symbolizes the sacred mountain, Maha Meru, belonging to the Hindu tradition. The word comes from the Sanskrit "caitya".

Erawan
Three-headed white elephant, the traditional mount of the deity Indra. As it is an albino, the white elephant is considered an incarnation of Buddha and is believed to be lucky.

Garuda
Mythical bird with an eagle's head portrayed while it is clutching two serpents. It is the traditional mount of the deity Visnu. The design of the garuda grasping the naga (the god of serpents) is believed to have the power to chase away evil spirits.

Kinnari
Mythological figure with a human face and birds' claws. If it represents a woman, it is referred to as a kinnari or kinnera, whereas if it represents a man, it is known as a kinnon.

Naga
Decorative design depicting stylized serpents, often used to decorate roofs. Legend has it that the king of serpents and enemy of the garuda lifted and protected Buddha who was meditating during a flood on earth lasting seven days and seven nights.

Prang
This name indicates the building of the prasad (see) when it is used for religious purposes. With an elegant, tapered outline, the prang comes from the towers of Khmer temples.

Prasad
Typical of Thai architecture, it is built according to a Greek cross plan and covered in numerous roofs. If the building is used for civil purposes, the roof ends in a tapered spire in the form of an arrow, or yot, similar to the royal crown; if, however, it is used for religious purposes, it takes on the shape of a prang (see).

Stupa
In ancient times it used to house Buddha's relics and therefore it was considered the most sacred building.
Subsequently, it was built to contain kings' relics and as a simple commemorative building.

Viharn
Similar in structure to a bot, it is not necessarily found in every wat (see). Also known as a vihara, it is a place of public worship and houses one or more statues of Buddha. In large sacred buildings, viharns are known by various names derived from the various statues of Buddha they contain.

Wat
A Thai temple, it is also the centre of the community's intellectual and religious life. It is not a place of worship in the western sense as no god is worshipped, but rather a complex of sacred buildings and monks' quarters used for prayer and meditation.

The Wat Phra Keo seen from the outer courtyard with the golden chedi in the foreground.

THE HISTORY OF THE CITY

Bangkok, the last capital of the Kingdom of Thailand, has a very recent history; it was in fact founded on the 20th April 1782. But in order to reach this date, one has to start much further back, at least one thousand years beforehand.

In fact, in 751, the Chinese empire was defeated by the state of Nan-Chao, situated in a region poetically called Yunnan, meaning "south of the clouds"; the inhabitants of this were of Thai origin and even though they were similar to the Chinese, their languages and physical charactristics differed. Their culture developed as from the first thousand year A.D.; during the XIth century, the Khmer epigraph quoted the Syam people for the first time. "Syam" means prisoners of war giving rise to the term Siam which was the traditional name for Thailand until recently.

The first capital of the country was Sukhothai, replaced by Ayutthaya which was devastated and destroyed by the Burmese fury in 1767. Two valiant generals then arrived: the first, Phya Taksin, reconquered the kingdom and had himself crowned king in Thonburi. Taksin then went mad and was assassinated; his place

was taken by the other general, Chao Phya Chakri, who had conquered the Cambodians. He considered it an ill omen to remain in Thonburi; therefore he moved the capital to the other bank of the river to a village inhabited by numerous Chinese merchants known as "village of the olives" or Ban Kok in the Thai language. 1782 was the foundation date of the new capital but also of the new dynasty of the Chakri which still reigns today. The first sovereign took the title of Rama I. Nine sovereigns in turn came to the Thai throne. The most significant for the country's history are Rama IV and Rama V, known by their first names of Mongkut and Chulalongkorn. Mongkut was also helped by literature and by cinematographic events in Hollywood; in fact he was the leading character in the memories of his children's English governess, Anne Leonowens, which were then filmed in "The King and I". but, apart from these fortunes, Rama IV was the first Thai sovereign to establish the first, vague contacts with Western culture and technology. After the Second World War, Bangkok was ever increasingly westernized, favoured in this aspect also by the American presence. In the vicinity of Vietnam, it encour-

aged and promoted a progressively higher and more modern standard of living.

But the ancient, exotic fascination of Bangkok in all its Eastern glory still remains intact. Even in its name, the Thai capital has managed to separate these two basic aspects of its very being. If Bangkok is the name with which it is known in the West, Krungtep or the "city of the angels" is only the first in a long, sweet series of names to have survived modernizaton, bringing the city back to its deeper Eastern reality.

Note: we report in full the name of the city in the thai language: Krungtep Maha Nakorn Amorn Ratanakosindra Mahindrayutthaya Mahadilokpop Nopraratana Rajdhani Burirom Udom Rajnivet Mahastan Amorn Pimarn Avtarn Satit Sakkhatutthaya Vishnukarn Prasit.

The collection of 52 statues of Buddha in the Cloister of Wat Benjamabopitr.

BONZES AND BUDDHISM

Characterized by their long, orange tunics, shaved heads and bowls for offerings consisting of a little rice and fruit which hang from their tunics, novices procure food by wandering around on foot begging in the countryside or along the modern streets of the city. The word bonze comes from the Japanese bōzu, meaning owner of the cell, or bōshi, meaning master in law. All of them can become bonzes: the majority of the population including the sovereign, do a novitiate in a monastery. The first meal is eaten at dawn and the second before midday: the bonzes dedicate their day to meditation and the study of sacred texts. Both bonzes and novices can neither touch nor approach a woman.

Buddhism, which is more a philosophy than a religion, nowadays boasts about six hundred million followers in the world. Strangely enough, it was not capable of taking a firm grip where it came into being in India.

Its founder, Siddharta Gautama, is one of the most important and fascinating figures in the history of mankind. He was born in 560 B.C. in a village on the boundary between India and Nepal and legend has it that his birth was accompanied by prodigious events. His mother Māyā died seven days after he was born because she who had conceived a Buddha had no remaining purpose in life. He spent his youth in luxury; then several times while walking outside his palace, a divinity revealed the sufferences of the world to him appearing in three different forms: a falling old man, a sick person and a corpse. Another day, the young prince met an ascetic begging with a bowl; he was moved by the serene, happy expression on this man's face. In fact, Gautama understood in that moment that the pleasures of life were vain and transitory and made his decision; at twenty-nine years of age, he abandoned his rich paternal palace and put on pilgrim's clothes. In the beginning he underwent severe penitence and

Bonze novices on the streets of Bangkok.

extreme mortification, even reaching the point of living on a grain of rice per day. Once he had reached the end of his strength, he realized that this extreme sacrifice would only have mortified his body but would not have led his spirit to enlightenment. He therefore went in for deep meditation and after seven years, one night in May, seated under a fig tree, he experienced the clairvoyance that revealed the four basic truths to him: the existence of pain, the origin of pain, the extinction of pain and the road that leads to the extinction of pain.

Having become Buddha in that moment, that is, having been enlightened, he started preaching to mankind; in 40 years of incessant pilgrimage, his doctrine was diffused, first by him and then by his disciples including his son Rāhula and his cousin Ānanda, among the masses in India and the neighbouring states.

In 480 B.C., Buddha fell ill in the town of Kusingara and died; the chronicles relates that a terrible earthquake shook the earth while his disciples were cremating his body.

Buddha in Thai sculpture

Thai sculpture has always represented the figure of Buddha to the point of being almost obsessive; he is portrayed in the various attitudes that symbolize the various stages in his life, which are about forty in number. His attitude is indicated above all by the position of his hands (mudra). The most frequent positions are given below.

Buddha meditating: seated in a yoga position, with his legs crossed and the palm of his hands turned upwards.

Buddha practicing asceticism; seated, with his hands crossed over his breast.

Buddha placating family quarrels: standing, his left hand along his body and his right hand lifted.

Buddha driving fear away: standing, with both hands lifted.

Buddha sleeping: that is, while he is entering Nirvana (the port of peace reached by him after his death), his left arm stretched out along his body and his feet placed one on top of the other.

5

◀ The small pavilion called Abhorn Pimok, which was used as a royal dressing-room for official ceremonies. The Chakri Residence looms up behind.

The façade of the Chakri Residence.

ROYAL PALACE

Built between 1782 and 1783, it is the main Thai royal residence and sprung up on the left bank of the river at the same time as the city of Bangkok. Its building complex covers an area of 218,400 square metres and is surrounded by 1900 metres of battlemented walls.

Its walls enclose not only goverment and representative buildings but also the Royal Chapel of the Emerald Buddha.

What is commonly known as the Great Palace in Bangkok consists of four parts: the Dusit Maha Prasad, the Chakri Residence, the Maha Montien and the Sivalaya garden.

The *Dusit Maha Prasad*, in exquisite Thai style, was built by Rama 1 for coronations and to act as a banqueting hall. It consists of a single, vast hall covered by five roofs placed one on top of the other and crowned by a spire-shaped prasad. It houses the throne in the form of a niche in the wall on which Rama 1 sat for the first time; in front of it, one can admire a new silver throne with mother-of-pearl inlay crowned by a 9 tier white canopy. Nowadays this hall is used only for exhibiting the mortal remains of members of the royal family.

The second building is the so-called *Chakri Residence* (or Chakri Maha Prasad), built in 1882 by English architects with an unusual mixture of styles; in fact, the Italian Renaissance style façade is crowned by roofs placed one on top of the other and decorated with pointed spires and naga serpents.

These are followed by the great Residence, or *Maha Montien*, the current residence of Rama Ill's successor. Tradition has it that once the king has been crowned he spends his first night here; only in this way can he

7

A view over the buildings forming
the Maha Montien.

The entrance door to the Audience
Chamber, or Amarinda.

take possession of the residence of his ancestors. From this building, we can admire the charming Audience Chamber, or Amarinda, where official ceremonies are held. It is worth noting the ancient throne in the shape of a ship where the curtains would then open and the monarch would appear in all his magnificent opulence, similar in all respects to Buddha to whom the gods relate him.

Some of the Ramas who came to the Thai throne are portrayed in one of the great halls; their portraits are by the Tuscan artist Galileo Chini who was invited by the sovereign himself to stay in Siam and whence he took back a rich artistic and anthropological documentation which can be found nowadays in a Florentine museum. Lastly the *Sivalaya Garden*, a vast lawn enhanced by elegant buildings, where court receptions are habitually held. In the centre of the garden, inside a marble chapel, one can admire the crystal Buddha, a small sculpture that some hunters found in the jungle to the north of Thailand and which they gave to King Rama II.

The Wat Phra Keo seen from the outer courtyard.

WAT PHRA KEO
(or Temple of the Emerald Buddha)

The Wat Phra Keo, or Temple of the Emerald Buddha, was built inside the palace walls in 1785 by Rama 1 as a royal chapel; unlike other temples, there are no monk's cells as, according to an ancient tradition, they cannot live inside a royal palace.

Completely restored in 1957 on the occasion of the 2,500th anniversary of the death of Buddha, it covers about 3,000 square metres, that is, one tenth of the entire surface of the Royal Palace. The monastery is surrounded by a covered gallery whose walls are painted with lively pictures portraying scenes from Ramakien; the latter is none other than the Thai version of the Indian epic poem, Ramayana, relating how Princess Sita, abducted by the demon Ravana, is finally joined and freed by her husband Rama leading an army of monkeys. The explanatory texts on the marble tablets were drawn up in Klong verse by King Chulalongkorn.

The enclosing wall is interrupted by six gates giving access to the temple. Twelve six metre high statues of demons stand guard over these doors; known as yaks in the Thai language, with their angry, threatening expressions and sharp teeth (in Thai iconography, this detail shows they belong to the forces of hell), these coloured giants add a note of excitement to our entrance into the splendid inner courtyard.

Of all the buildings inside the circle of walls, the most important and sacred is the bot, that houses the most venerated statue in the whole country, the famous *Emerald Buddha*.

The rectangular-shaped bot covers almost the entire southern part of the sacred area; it is covered by a roof on several tiers crowned by naga serpents and numerous little bells that ring softly in the gentle brezze. The outside walls of the bot are covered in blue enamel and inlaid with mother of pearl; along the base runs a frieze

9

◀ *A gigantic yak standing guard over the sacred enclosure.*

The entrance to the Wat Phra Keo with the yaks.

of 112 gilt garudas gripping naga snakes. Under the colonnade, the three doors of access are guarded by three couples of bronze lions, probably cast by Thai artists who wanted to imitate khmer style lions.

Inside the bot and at the top of the gilt stairs, the Emerald Buddha venerated by all Buddhists can be found inside a gold altar that symbolizes the mythical flying chariots of the Hindu gods. In fact, this sixty centimetre high statue is a single block of jade, which, according to legend, was created by the gods themselves for the Ceylonese king of serpents. It is portrayed in a sitting position, with the right leg supported by the left leg. The statue, which is dressed in different apparel according to the various seasons (blue sequins for the rainy season, gold and diamonds for the hot season and only gold cloth for the dry season) has had a very eventful history; the exact date is not known but it would appear that it was sculpted in North Thailand, approximately during the XVth century, that is, at the end of the Chieng Saen period. It was first mentioned

in a chronicle dating back to 1436, when it was found, covered in plaster, in a chedi of the Temple of Chiang Rai, in North Thailand. During a violent hurricane, the chedi was destroyed and the statue was taken away in a bad state of repair. One day a monk realized that the plaster was peeling off the Buddha's nose and that another green statue was peeping through from underneath. Once all the plaster had been removed, the jade statue came to light and was immediately venerated by the entire population. As soon as he heard about it, the king of nearby Chiang Mai set one of his elephants to bring him back the statuette but the animal, as if driven by a mysterious instinct, headed in the direction of Lampang thrice without taking the road back to Chiang Mai; nobody dared oppose this wish of the gods and so the statue remained in Lampang for 32 years. In 1468 the effigy was sent to Chiang Mai, where it was exhibited in the niche of the large stupa called Chedi Luang; when the town passed under the dominion of Laos, the statue was taken to Luang Prabang

View of the bot.

Some of the 12 "salas" that surround the bot; these small pavilions are used as dormitories for pilgrims during large ceremonies or to house monks' offerings.

*View over some of the eight ornate
inscribed pillars that circumscribe
the bot and are called "bai sema".*

*The bell-tower on the south side of
the Wat Phra Keo enclosure.*

*On the following pages: two views
of the bot.*

Detail of the crowning part of the bot.

The entrance to the bot under the colonnade, with the doors guarded by couples of bronze lions.

Detail of the bot's wall, with the frieze formed by a long row of garudas.

Detail of the garudas.

Two views of the enclosure for offerings in front of the bot.

The side of the bot, with inscribed pillars and small temples.

Detail of the pediment of a sala.

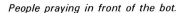

and in 1564 to the new capital, Vientiane, where it remained for 214 years. In 1778, during the war against Laos, General Chakri conquered Vientiane and so the statue finally returned to Thailand. It was taken to Thonburi, where it remained until 22nd March 1784, when with a solemn, magnificent ceremony it was taken to the Temple of Wat Phra Keo.

In front of the altar, a small bronze statue by Mongkut (before he became Rama IV), portrays Buddha as Phra Samputtha Panni. To the right and left, two three metre high bronze statues covered in gold and precious stones are the symbolic incarnation of Buddha with his hands placed in such a way as to drive away fear; they were dedicated by Rama III to his predecessors Rama I and Rama II. The modern paintings on the wall depict episodes from Jatakas, the legends of Buddha's 550 previous lives. In fact, according to the Buddhist religion, the apparition on earth of the historic Buddha, Siddharta Gautama, was preceded by that of 550 other Buddhas before his time.

On leaving the bot with its magic atmosphere inducive to prayer and meditation and interior full of shadows, we are stunned by the bright colours of the Wat Phra Keo. We are dazzled by the sparkle of the glass mosaics and astounded by a very rich décor which has successfully avoided being kitsch or excessive.

The *Prasad Phra Tepbidorn*, or Royal Pantheon, stands out on account of its beauty and elegance on the large raized terrace nextdoor. It was originally built in 1856 to house the emerald Buddha, but is judged too small for large ceremonies to be held there. In the shape of a Greek cross, with it roof crowned by a yellow prang, it houses the standing statues of the first eight kings of the Chakri dynasty, from Rama I to Rama VIII; the first four are dressed in national costume while the others are wearing uniforms.

In front of the Pantheon, two large gilt stupas and numerous gold statues of mythological figures with human faces and birds'claws are referred to as Kinnari if they represent a woman and Kinnon if they represent a man; legend has it that they lived in the equally mythical Himavanta forest at the foot of the Himalayas. Behind the Pantheon stands a square building, the Library or *Maha Mandapa*, which contains the sacred Buddhist scriptures. Of these texts, the most important one is the Tripitaka (triple basket), kept in a casket encrusted in mother of pearl on black lacquer and drawn up in 1788 in the Pali language and Thai Writing; this code is the written record of Buddha's preachings. The large chedi to the east on the terrace

A partial view of the gold stupa.

The Pantheon seen from the bot.

Façade of the Pantheon, or Prasad
Phra Thepbidorn.

Overview of the Pantheon and gold stupa. ▶

Detail of one of the numerous ▶
rockeries decorated with Chinese
statues and bonsai plants.

◄ *The entrance
to the Pantheon.*

The gold stupa.

◀ One of the prangs
along the wall
surrounding
the Wat Phra Keo.

Detail of a yak.

◀ *Flight of steps leading to the Pantheon and one of the two gold stupas.*

Detail of the demon caryatid supporting the gold stupa.

was erected by Mongkut along the lines of a destroyed chedi in Ayutthaya and it is completely covered in gold leaf.

The grey stone model in the Temple of Angkor Wat alongside it is a reminder of when Cambodgia was a vassal state of Thailand. The building of Wiharn Yod, with it roof superbly decorated in ceramics and porcelain stands in front of it.

A further two buildings complete the Wat Phra Keo complex: the Viharn Phra Nak (in the north west corner) and the Supplementary Library, or Ho Phra Monthien Tam, in the opposite corner. The former is a small mausoleum containing the cinerary urns of members of the royal family whereas the latter is said to have the most beautiful façade in the whole of Thailand.

The eight prangs along the eastern side of the Wat Phra Keo, covered in ceramics and encrusted in mosaics, are traditionally supposed to symbolize the eight planets of Buddhism and represent the eight most significant elements of the religion: Buddha, teaching (Dharma), the monastic community (Sangha), the ancient Buddhist disciples (Bhikshuni), the monks (Pacchekabodhi), the kings (Chakravarti), the past Buddha (Bodhisattva) and the future Buddha (Maitraya).

These three photos depict statues of kinnaris.

◄ Statues of kinnaris in female form and kinnons in male form.

The demon caryatids supporting the stupa.

A lotus flower in an oriental ceramic vase.

Following pages: charming view of the Library of the Wat Phra Keo and the imposing chedi built by Mongkut and covered in gold leaf.

The inner courtyard of the Wat Po.

The bot inside the Wat Po. ▶

WAT PO

When this temple (whose real name is Wat Phra Jetubon) was built, Bangkok had not yet come into existence and Ayutthaya was the capital.

Today the Wat Po is not only the oldest temple in Bangkok, but also the largest (with its eight hectares) and one of the most venerated. Considered the first University in Thailand, it is divided in half by the street. The southern part is a real monastic town, inhabited by about three hundred monks, with schools, a library, chapels and old houses. The northern part, open to tourists, contains the sacred buildings. Access is gained through one of the sixteen doors that open along the long enclosing walls, protected by fierce-looking stone statues.

Inside, four large chedis represent the first four kings of the Chakri dynasty, from the green mosaic one of Rama I to the blue mosaic one of Rama IV; the gallery surrounding the bot houses a further 91 chedis, of which 71 small ones contain the ashes of numerous descendants of the royal family and 20 smaller ones house Buddha's relics.

Two galleries, featuring 394 statues of Buddha seated, surround the bot, closed by huge doors in teak encrusted in mother of pearl which are without doubt the most beautiful in the entire city. Near the bot, a large "lingam" or black phallus is an example of the influence of Hinduism over Buddhism: in fact, the phallus, symbol of the fertility of the Hindu god Shiva, is always decorated in flower necklaces and wet with holy water by desirous of having children.

The Wat Po is also known as the temple of Buddha stretched out; in fact, inside the Viharn Phra Non, one can find the largest statue of Buddha stretched out in the whole of Thailand. Buddha is portrayed the moment in which he is about to enter into Nirvana, his head supported on his right and his left arm hanging at this side. Built in brick covered in gold leaf, it is 45 metres long and 15 metres high. The sole of his feet facing westwards are inlaid with 108 mother of pearl tablets arranged in numerous square panels, each with its own precise symblic or religious meaning, and through which one can recongize the real Buddha. The most frequently reproduced one is Dharma Chakra, which represents the "Course of Law".

The statue of Buddha and a detail of
his feet inlaid with mother of pearl.

View of the inner courtyard of the ▶
Wat Po.

The gigantic statues in the Wat Po ▶
were cut out of the blocks of stone
used to ballast trading ships
sent to China. Tradition has it that
this tall figure with a hat portrays
Marco Polo.

One of the Buddhas inside the Wat ▶
Po, seated above the spirals of the
naga serpent whose seven heads
loom up behind.

Two external views of the Wat Traimit.

The gold statue of Buddha inside the temple.▶

WAT TRAIMIT
(or Temple of the Golden Buddha)

The Wat Traimit, whose name means "temple of three friends" is located in the heart of the Chinese district. The sacred temple features a large bot, a crematorium and some viharas. What the temple is rightly most famous for can be found in a simple two storey building: a three metre high, pure gold statue of Buddha seated weighing five and a half tons. Nowadays, its value would be over 15 million American dollars.

There is quite a tale to tell around this statue, a fine example of XIIIth century Sukhothai style. It was discovered by chance in 1954 thanks to torrential rains which poured down on the town. In fact, the gold Buddha had been concealed under a thick layer of plaster to hide it from Burmese eyes during the Ayutthaya looting; in this way, the precious relic remained hidden for over two hundred years, until the day in which, on account of the rain, the plaster broke away, revealing the mass of gold in all its splendour, while it was being transported by workers.

External views of the Marble Temple.

WAT BENJAMABOPITR

Better known as Marble Temple, it was built in about 1900 by King Chulalongkorn. From the stylistic point of view, it is a breaking point with previous architecture in Bangkok. Pillars, balustrades, walls, staircases, floor and even imposing lions standing guard at the entrance are carved in marble, which the monarch imported specially from Carrara.

A solemn staircase leads up to the bot where one can admire in front of the altar a copy of Buddha Jinnaraj,

The garden with the canal to the
side of the Marble Temple.

The Buddha seated in front of the altar.

cast in 1300 in Phitsanulok and whose clog contains
the ashes of Chulalongkorn.

The cloister houses a rare collection of 52 bronze
statues of Buddha, representing the main phases of
Buddhist art. Slightly larger than life size, these statues
are either originals or reproductions of works scattered
throughout the country. Buddha walking in Sukhothai
is quite outstanding, but the most amazing one is without a doubt the Gandhara statue portraying Buddha
fasting, whose original is to be found in the museum of
Lahore.

The sacred buildings are separated from the monks'
buildings by a canal with numerous turtles, a gift from
believers desirous of praise.

A partial view of the Wat Rajabopit.

Detail of the temple decoration.

View from above of the Wat Rajanadda.

WAT RAJABOPIT

Built in 1863 by Mongkut the temple, which over-looks the characteristic klong, is entirely covered in Chinese ceramics with floral designs. The doors inlaid with figures of smiling soldiers dressed in Western style uniforms are very typical.

In the garden the royal cemetery contains the tombs of the family of King Chulalongkorn and his successors. Every funeral monument is in a different style: they go from European Neo-Gothic styles to Khmer styles and from Hindu styles to Thai styles, and so on.

WAT RAJANADDA

The "temple of the royal grandson" was built in 1846 by Rama 111 for Princess Somanat Wattana Wadi. The originality of these temples lies in their "Dhama Chedi Loha Prasat" architecture, whose origins are unknown and of which it is the only example in Thailand. Also called the Third Castle in the World, it consists of 5 tapering floors, on which 36 pavilions with spire-shaped turrets rest.

View of the chedi at the top of the Gold Mountain.

WAT SAKHET

At the time that Thonburi was still the capital, a small monastery called Wat Sakal stood here. Legend has it that one day in 1782 General Chakri stopped here to purify himself on his way back to Thonburi, where he was to be crowned as Rama 1; the temple was subsequently enlarged and its name changed to Wat Sakhet, meaning "hair washing".

The western part of the building is formed by the Phu Chao Thong, that is, by the Gold Mountain, an artificial eighty metre high hill which has become the highest point in the town, whence one can see the low houses of Bangkok, soaring temple spires, gold chedis and elegant, harmonious roof tops. By means of a spiral staircase at 318 decrees, one can reach the roof where a large gilt chedi towers above, housing as a precious relic one of Buddha's bones found in 1894 between India and Nepal.

The terrace of the chedi is open to the public during November, when the solemn ceremonies of Wat Sakhet are held: on that occasion, there is an endless procession of hundreds of coloured lamps along the whole of Gold Mountain.

45

This characteristic means of transport to Bangkok is called sanlo, but it is commonly known as tuk tuk, clearly referring to the sound it makes when it is in operation. It is practically a large tricycle equipped with a seat in the rear and covered by a light canopy in plastic-coated cloth. No more than three passengers can travel on it at the same time. The driver manages to squeeze past and to steer a middle course in the chaotic traffic of Bangkok with amazing skill and audacity; on a level with the classic tour on tranquil klongs, this is a worthwhile experience in Bangkok.

◄ Panoramas over Bangkok from the top of the Wat Sakhet.

Following pages
Some pictures taken in the animated Chinese district that gravitates around the main thoroughfare called Yaowarat Road.

ERAWAN SHRINE

Of all the countless shrines in Bangkok, this shrine located right in front of the Erawan Hotel is one of the most popular and crowded, both during the day and at night.

It is dedicated to Siva, one of the most important gods in the Hindu religion, who presides over creation and fertility. Popular devotion attributes great power to it and, for every favour granted, believers offer it statuettes of inlaid elephants, garlands of orchids and sweetly-perfumed jasmine or sticks of incense. As Siva is also the god of dancing, who created the universe dancing, it is not a rare sight to see classic works of Thai art offered in honour of the god through whom a wish has been granted.

In these photos, some pictures of ▶ preparation for dances at Erawan Shrine.

A woman selling orchids and a typical oriental shop in Chinese district.

Exterior of Jim Thompson's house.

The dining-room with ceramic of the Ming dynasty.

The bedroom.

The "mice's house".

Shop-window with ceramic and
enamel vases.

The patio leading to the house.

JIM THOMPSON'S HOUSE

In one of Bangkok's most noisy districts, at the bottom of a quiet soi, one comes across Jim Thompson's Thai house, an oasis of peace and serenity along the Klong Saen Saep. James Thompson was born in Delaware in 1906. Trained as an architect, he came to Thailand as a volunteer with the American army; having arrived in Bangkok two days after the armistice, he remained as an O.S.S. official and once he had left the secret service, he decided to stay on in Bangkok forever. Thompson immediately became interested in silk weaving by hand; at the time, only certain families on the Klong Bang Krua, in the heart of old Bangkok, knew the art. He gave such a boost to this industry that he founded the Thai Silk Company, making Thai silk world famous. A very refined man with exquisite taste, Thompson wanted to build himself a house expressing the best Thai domestic architecture. In order to do so, he put together seven different buildings in teak coming from different places and all at least two hundred years old; he had them dismounted and reassembled exactly where they are now in accordance with the

procedures adopted by the original builders. For instance, the roof tiles were fired in Ayutthaya according to an ancient custom. The only concession he made to modern comfort was the installation of electricity in the XVIIIth and XIXth century chandeliers from the old palaces in Bangkok. Also when inaugurating his house, Thompson wanted to follow the customs of what he by then considered his second fatherland and on a spring day in 1959 decreed propitious by astrologers, he moved house.

Inside his home, Thompson was surrounded by a fabulous collection of Asiatic art; so much so that one evening after dinner, the famous writer Somerset Maugham said to him: "Not only do you have beautiful things, but what is more endearing, you have displayed them so beautifully".

On the 27th March 1967, during a trip to the Cameron Highlands in Malaysia, Jim Thompson mysteriously disappeared without leaving any trace.

Despite searches, there was no further sign of his whereabouts. In 1976 the Foundation dedicated to him was established; it was decided to open his house and collection to the public, giving all his earnings to a school for the blind.

Jim Thompson's heirs have left it just as it was: precious Chinese Ming white and blue ceramics; wooden Burmese statues; rare specimens of Bencharong ("five colours", a molticoloured porcelain that the Chinese produced only for export to Thailand); a dining table on which Rama V used to play cards ad rare pictures of Buddha.

View of the Damnoen Saduak klong,▶
where the famous floating market is held.

A partial view of a klong.

A wooden foot-bridge over a klong.

THE WATERWAYS
(Klongs)

Once upon a time, the city life along the canals on klongs was such a hive of activity that Bangkok was called the Venice of the East. In fact, as in the case of Venice, the canals here have traced, determined and conditioned its life and development. Here everything takes place on the water: daily life, cultural exchanges and traffic. As a rule, people living along the klongs use them to wash themselves and do their washing. Once upon a time, the klongs were far more numerous than they are today; subsequently, due to the continuous increase of the number of cars circulating, the majority of canals were reclaimed.

It is an unforgettable experience to climb aboard a "hang yao", or boat with a long tail, and to slowly travel up the Chao Phaya. In this way, one has the opportunity of seeing the European nineteenth century style buildings along the banks of the river alongside modern embassies, typical Thai houses next to a deco-

On this and the following pages,
pictures of the characteristic floating
market which is held along the
Damnoen Saduak klong.

rated Chinese pagoda and the spires of the Wat Phra
Keo rising up into the air behind the immobile skyline
of temples.

There are incessant comings and goings on the river;
boats packed with tourists; Thai boats with a family
cooking and having a meal aboard and boats belonging to vendors and buyers, full of fruit and vegetables,
not to mention rice and dry fish, cocunuts and
bananas.

From crowded Chao Phaya to the spectacular Klong
Saen Saep and to the smallest, most insignificant canal,
these waterways represent a world animated by a completely different way of life, which cannot fail to fasci-
nate Westerners.

FLOATING MARKET

At about sixty kilometers from Bangkok, along the
Klong Damnoen Saduak in the province of Ratcha-
buri, the characteristic floating market is held. Unlike
other markets nearer the capital and due to its dis-
tance, this market has remained quite authentic and
complete, giving us a vague idea of what life along the
canals was like many decades ago. The markest of
Damnoen Saduak is quite rightly famous on account
of the variety and quality of products traded, especially
fruit from nearby orchards, including the large grape-
fruit known as Sam-O.

Two of the most common sights in Thailand are cobra and mongoose fighting and snake charming, when the snake charmer grasps the serpent with his bare hands to remove its poison. The cobra, which is very common in Thailand, is distinguished by the fact that it raises its hood. Its poison, which is extremely strong, is a pale yellow colour.

The Chedi of Nakhon Pathom, the highest Buddhist monument in the world, the gilt statue of Buddha and the garden.

NAKHON PATHOM

We have documentary evidence that the city of Nakhon Pathom is ancient and dates back to over two thousand years ago.

Tradition has it that two Indian missionary monks by the names of Sona and Uttara went there to teach the Buddhist doctrine. However, the Thai Buddhist tradition maintains that during his pilgrimage, Buddha took rest in the very place where the Nakhon Pathom Chedi stands today and that later on King Mongkut decided to rebuild this palace where Buddhism was manifested for the first time in his country.

The gigantic chedi is not only the most venerated chedi in the whole of Thailand (whence its name Chedi Phra Phatom comes), but it is also the highest Buddhist monument in the world: on an original 40 metre high hemispheric stupa, in fact, a chedi in the traditional Siamese shape was placed, until it reached the incredible height of 127 metres! Covered in gilt tiles, it has a diameter of 98 metres and access is gained by an imposing staircase looking upwards to a viharn dominated by a gilt statue of Buddha standing up with his right hand lifted and flanked by four smaller statues in gold.

The Rose Garden lake and a view of a canal.

ROSE GARDEN

On the banks of the Katchine river, the Rose Garden or Suan Sam Phran is a huge park with over twenty thousand rose-bushes, numerous other species of flowers and plants, beautifully kept gardens, five hotels, swimming-pools and examples of Thai architecture. Everything that Thailand can offer in the field of handicrafts and folklore is on display there; every afternoon a spectacle of traditional dances, Thai wrestling and cock fighting takes place in a large covered amphitheatre.

Following pages: a view of the garden, the show with elephants and two dancers in their ornate costumes.

The Aisawan Thi Paya pavilion ▶
reflected in the lake.

BANG PA IN

The summer residence of the royal family as long as nearby Ayutthaya remained the capital, Bang Pa In reflects the Thai monarchy's admiration for European taste in its unusual buildings.

When Prasad Thong came to the throne in 1630, he already possessed on the Chao Phaya the island of Bang Pa In, where he had a temple, the Wat Chumpon Nikayaram, built; he then built a palace surrounded by a lake that the sovereign had lengthened until it was 400 metres long.

Having fallen to ruin when the court moved to Bangkok, the Bang Pa In complex was rediscovered by King Mongkut who came up with the idea of using a steamer to travel more quickly along the river. Of all the buildings that form Bang Pa In, one is immediately struck by the elegance and refinement of the pavilion that rises up in the middle of the lake, the *Aisawan Thi Paya*, a typical example of Siamese architecture, with its slender columns that support the three storey pagoda roof covered in painted tiles and crowned in the centre by a soaring spire.

The Vahat Chamrun, built in the style of a royal Chinese palace, was donated by the wealthiest Chinese community in Bangkok. Another building recalls Queen Sunantha, wife of King Chulalongkorn, who drowned in the lake with three children in 1880. None of his servants could save him because there was a death penalty for those who touched a member of the royal family.

A ferry-boat (or an unusual cableway that travels incessantly up and down the river) takes one to the other bank of the Chao Phaya, where one comes across the *Wat Nivet Dammapravat*, which leaves one astounded because of its Neo-Gothic church appearance. It was built by Chulalongkorn for the monks of the Dhammayuttika sect. It houses a sculpture by a royal prince, Pradit Varakarn, who is said to have been an expert sculptor during the reigns of Mongkut and Chulalongkorn.

A bodhi tree in Bang Pa In.

The interior of the Wat Nivet
Dammapravat, with its
unconventional Neo-Gothic
appearance.

Along the Menam Chao Phya.

The characteristic cableway that passes the river in Bang·Pa In.

In Thailand, dancing, the theatre and music are closely connected.
The leading traditional shadow play, or Nang, is followed by the mask play, or Khon, whose subjects are inspired by mythology and legends of Hindu origin, such as Ramakien or Mahabharata, and which is distinguished by elaborate costumes and high hats. Mention must also be made of the Lakon, religious ballet and essentially an art of the court. Furthermore, there is still evidence of folk-dances from Thailand's farthest corners, such as the Ramwong, a type of round with greatly simplified steps that are perpetuated and kept alive by numerous impromptu groups.
The dancers start their training very young, at six years of age or eight at the very latest. Thai dancing features roles for men, women, demons and monkeys. Dancers are submitted to a strict code of gestures. Nothing is left to chance; everything has a precise meaning, from the cupping of the hand, which is lengthened, creating a dramatic effect, by long gilt metal nails, to the twisting of the ankle and from the bending of the neck to the casting of a glance.

Taken at a popular show.

AYUTTHAYA

The first nucleus of Ayutthaya, whose name means "mild" appears to have been founded by the Khmer during the XIth century as the outpost of their kingdom. Two centuries later, it became the frontier post of U Thong, a vassal state of Sukhothai.

In 1347, due to an epidemic, the reigning prince chose to abandon U Thong and chose a new capital where the Lop Buri flows into the Chao Phaya at Ayutthaya, which annexed Sukhothai at the end of the XIVth century, becoming a powerful state.

As from this moment for at least four centuries, Ayutthaya lived an era of incomparable glory. From 1350 to 1767, the year in which it fell, thirty-three sovereigns of different dynasties in turn sat on the throne of Ayutthaya. Heirs to the Thai tradition of Sukhotai and to the Khmer cultural heritage of Angkor, who they had conquered and destroyed in 1431, the sovereigns embellished the city with grandiose monuments and elegant buildings, centralized the capital's administration and protected the arts.

The Ayutthaya era is the culmination of Thai culture. In literature, court poetry came into being; in sculpture, Buddha was portrayed differently in princely garments. The city and state, above all, opened their doors to trade and economic exchanges, as can be seen from the reports of astonished European travellers. The Portuguese were the first to arrive in 1511, followed by the Dutch in 1605 and then the English and Danes, terminating with the French in 1662. It set up a flourishing trade with China, which concentrade mainly on silk and porcelain.

It was during this period that the Greek Constantine Phaulkon appeared on the scene; an adventurer who managed to become prime minister at the Thai court, he had Louis XIV send him a garrison of French soldiers in 1687; however, the people soon realized that the foreigners' main aim was not to establish business relations but to conquer the country. After a bloody revolt, the foreign army was expelled and Phaulkon was executed. After this episode, Thailand preferred to remain isolated for at least 150 years.

The Kingdom of Ayutthaya continued to fight its minor and major battles against border states; in the incessant struggles for dominion of the peninsula, Burma was always the most implacable enemy of the Thai state. In 1572, the Burmese managed to conquer Ayutthaya for the first time, but after fifteen years King Naresuen or Narai managed to free the state from the invader; from then onwards he was worshipped as a god. Two centuries later, the Burmese armies returned and after two years of siege, on the 7th April 1967, the capital was forced to surrender. What was called the "pearl of Siam" was sacked and razed to the ground: gold and jewelry were plundered, statues knocked down and highly important treasures such as literary and religious documents were burnt. The materials used later on to construct Thonburi and Bangkok were taken from the ruins of Ayutthaya.

Exterior of the Wat Phanam Choeng.

Two chedis in the Wat Yai Chai Mongkol.

The long file of Buddhas seated in ▶
the temple.

The large statue of Buddha stretched ▶
out inside the temple.

WAT PHANAM CHOENG

Previous page:

This temple which directly overlooks the Chao Phaya is said to have been founded in 1324, when Ayutthaya was not yet the capital.

Completely renovated in 2397 A.B. by Rama IV, the temple houses an enormous statue of Buddha seated; 19 metres high, it is so impressive that it seems to support the ceiling of the building.

Hundreds of small niches, which must have housed votive statues, open out in the temple's internal walls. For many years, this building was the Chinese trader's favourite place of worship where they would come to pray before undertaking long and dangerous journeys.

WAT YAI CHAI MONGKOL

Situated to the south east of the city, this temple known as Wat Chao Phya Thai is one of the oldest buildings; it was built in 1357 by King Rama Thibodi who wanted to consecrate it to a sect of monks, Pa Kaeo, who on their return from Ceylon dedicated themselves to meditation. Inside the surrounding walls, a huge statue of Buddha stretched out is paid homage to and worshipped daily by believers.

An imposing chedi rises up behind the fortified wall; it was built by King Naresuen in memory of his own personal victory astride an elephant over the commander of the Burmese army, Suphan Buri. It is said that the king's spirit dwells in the chedi, which is still surrounded today by numerous statues of Buddha seated; for centuries, believers have been coming here to ask the spirit of the victorious sovereign for advice through two priests.

◄The imposing chedi that dominates
the Wat Yai Chai Mongkol.

A statue of Buddha leaning against
a prang in the Wat Mahathat.

WAT MAHATHAT

Magnificent ruins are all that remain today of this temple which tradition has it was founded by King Ramesuen in 1384. It was dominated by a 46 metre high prang, which was lifted to a height of 56 metres in 1633; after it was destroyed by the Burmese, all that remained of it was its base, which is still standing today. During an excavation campaign in 1956, in the midst of the prang ruins, access to a secret chamber containing very valuable artistic and religious treasures was discovered in 1956: a golden casket containing a relic of Buddha; votive tablets in gold; bracelets; small plates in fine porcelain; necklaces in gold, rubies and rock crystal, and lanterns. One of the most outstanding pieces was an unusual marble fish containing various everday utensils, all of which are in gold. All these precious finds can be admired nowadays in the National Museum of Bangkok, bearing witness to the refined culture that developed in Ayutthaya during the four centuries in which the city was the capital of the kingdom.

At the entrance to the temple, a relief model of the city only gives us a vague idea of its original size: the surrounding fortified walls, the Pom Maha Chai, the fortress that rose at the north-east end and of which only a trace remains today; the brick citadel known as Pom Phat, built on the opposite corner, and gardens.

Popular devotion in the Wat Mahathat.

Two pictures of the breathtaking ruins of the Wat Mahathat.

The entrance to the Wat Raj Burana. ▶

The central prang framed by the ▶
main entrance.

A view from above of the entrance ▶
to the Wat Raj Burana.

The red bricks of the Wat Mahathat
stand out from the green of the
lawn.

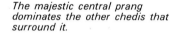
The majestic central prang dominates the other chedis that surround it.

Detail of a viharn that opens onto the prang.

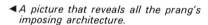
◀ A picture that reveals all the prang's imposing architecture.

WAT RAJ BURANA

The Wat Raj Burana stands right in front of the Wat Mahathat, its elegant, imposing counterpoint. It was built by King Boromaraja II in 1424 on the cremation site of his two older brothers, Ay and Yo, both of whom died in battle and whose ashes are kept in the two chedis at the interesection of the two streets. Another chedi, the Sri Suriyothai, recalls the courageous queen who sacrificed her life in 1563 to save the life of her husband Maha Chakrapat during a furious battle against the Burmese fought with elephants.

The temple is dominated by the large central prang, which is in a excellent state of preservation. Originally the large terrace that supports the prang featured four large chedis at the four corners and smaller chedis along its entire perimeter. Having reached the summit, you go down to the crypt, where over one hundred thousand votive tablets were discovered and where one can admire fragments of mural paintings dating back to the time in which Ayutthaya started to expand its dominion.

WAT SRI SAMPHET

It was the most beautiful, important and largest temple in the old capital. It was to be found inside the enclosing walls of the Wang Luang royal palace; therefore, there were no monks' cells. It was similar to the Wat Phra Keo in Bangkok in that it was the king's private chapel and is perhaps the best expression of the town's elegant architecture at the peak of its glory.

The three large chedis along its terrace recall the first three kings of Ayutthaya. In 1492, Rama Thibodi II had the first two built: the east chedi to house the ashes of his father, King Boroma Trailokanat, and the central chedi for the ashes of his older brother, Boromaraja III. The third chedi was erected in 1540 by Boromaraja Noh Buddhangkum to house the ashes of Rama Thibodi II. It was the builder of the first two chedi, Rama Thibodi II who had the large viharn built to insert an imposing statue of Buddha standing; it is 16 metres high and covered by 263 kilograms of pure gold. When the Burmese conquered Ayutthaya, the first thing they tried to do was to take possession of the

◄ *The three large chedis of the Wat Sri Samphet that recall the first three kings of Ayutthaya.*

On these pages, three views of the ruins of the Wat Sri Samphet.

gold and so they set fire to the chapel, transforming the whole temple in a huge brazier with a result that the gold melted and the temple collapsed. What remained of this statue was then taken to Bangkok by Rama I, who had a large chedi built inside the Wat Po to house the remaining fragments of the statue.

Countless other statues of Buddha, some of which are very famous, were brought to light from the temple ruins. These include a number of small statues in gold, silver and lead. A series of small stupas were also found inserted inside one another: the smallest in glass contained ashes which one supposes belong to Buddha.

The large bot of the Wat Na Phra Meru.

The Buddha seated of the Dvaravati period inside the small temple.

WAT NA PHRA MERU

Old documents provide information on this temple; they do not refer to its foundation date, which is still unknown, but the period in which it was restored, that is, between 1733 and 1759, during the reign of Boroma Kot. Its importance lies in the fact that it was salvaged from the Burmese destruction of Ayutthaya. This has enabled us to admire the large bot surrounded by columns (one of the largest in the city) intact and the small viharn with its magnificent richly sculpted doors. Two statues of Buddha are kept in this sacred architectural complex. The statue in the main temple is large and dressed in regal, highly ornate apparel according to Mahayana tradition (the "Great Vehicle", that is, the form of Buddhism that incorporates many aspects of ancient Hinduism) whereas the other small, black, stone statue kept in the small temple portrays Buddha seated Western style and not in a yoga position and is a splendid example of the Dvaravati period (VI-XI century). The perfect, harmonious proportions of the body and the expressive face manifesting inner calm are the outstanding features of this Buddha which was found among the ruins of Wat Mahathat, but it is generally believed that they come from Nakhon Pathom.

Phra Mane Square and the façade of
the Phra Mongkol Bopitr Viharn.

The bronze statue of Buddha seated
inside the temple.

VIHARN PHRA MONGKOL BOPITR

Once upon a time, solemn cremation ceremonies of members of the royal family were held in Phra Mane Square. Nowadays, coloured stands and small restaurants attract tourists who come to visit this temple with their typical products: large woven straw hats, which are the typical handicraft of Ayutthaya, painted fabrics, silks and bronze objects.

The temple is a recent construction; it was rebuilt along the lines of its original architecture in 1956 by the prime minister, Phibul Songgram, to house the large bronze statue of Buddha which the Burmese did not manage to take away and which, once it was abandoned by Ayutthaya, was left in the open air for centuries, exposed to inclement weather and damage.

This is the largest statue of Buddha in a sitting position in the whole of Thailand; 22 and a half meters high and originally covered in gold robbed from the Burmese, it was probably cast between 1448 and 1486, that is, during the reign of Boroma Trailokanat. In any case, the U Thong and Sukhotai periods have clearly influenced its style.

During the final restoration, hundreds of votive statuettes were discovered inside the statue.

A typical means of transport.

In this and following pages, four pictures of the Crocodile Farm.

CROCODILE FARM

"A successful combination between wild life conservation and a business enterprise": this is what is written in the leaflets advertising the Crocodile Farm at Samut Prakarn, thirty kilometers from Bangkok on the road to Pattaya.

Founded in 1950 by Utai Yongporapakorn, nowadays the Samut Prakarn Farm is over three thousand strong, including South American alligators, Nile crocodiles, aligators and all varieties of Thai fresh water and sea water fauna.

The dual purpose of the farm is to preserve and continue the species on the one hand and to supply high quality skins to the international market on the other.

Every day an exciting spectacle takes part on the farm with the trainers joining the crocodiles in a dam. A zoo featuring various types of elephant, tigers, gibbons and poisonous snakes is flanked by elegant boutiques selling handbags, shoes, belts and wallets to tourists.

View from above of the bay onto which Pattaya faces.

The sea-front and beach at Pattaya.

PATTAYA

Until twenty years ago, this place about 150 kilometers east of Bangkok was a small, tranquil fishing village with three kilometres of beach mainly visited by Thais from the capital, who were prepared to put up with the discomfort of rough roads to dive into the crystal clear water of the bay. Nowadays Pattaya is one of the most fashionable beaches, assiduously frequented not only by Thais but above all by tourists who come here to rest, distracted by the numerous water and equestrian sports and enthralled by the intense, varied night life in Bangkok.

The boom of Pattaya started at the beginning of the sixties when it was frequented by American pilots from the nearby base of Sattahip during the Vietnam war. The large tourist development that involved the whole of Thailand took place at the same time. In a matter of two years, the quiet fishing bay changed radically: luxury hotels shot up along the main coast road; restaurants serving local and Western cuisines were built one next to the other and sports facilities were increased on the palm shaded beaches.

Open air cafés, which were simple kiosks run by groups of girls, sprung up like mushrooms while jewelry shops offering sapphires, rubies and emeralds were even more numerous.

About an hour's sailing from Pattaya, boats, featuring glass keels so as to be able to admire the coral-covered sea bed, take one to *Koh Larn*, also known as coral island, where, apart from the natural beauty of unspoilt, uncontaminated sea, one can taste the specialities of the Thai cuisine, especially crab and crayfish.

Two pictures of the beach in Pattaya.

The swimming pool at one of the numerous, modern hotels in Pattaya.

The lotus flower, symbol of Thailand.

Four pictures of the frenetic night life in Pattaya.

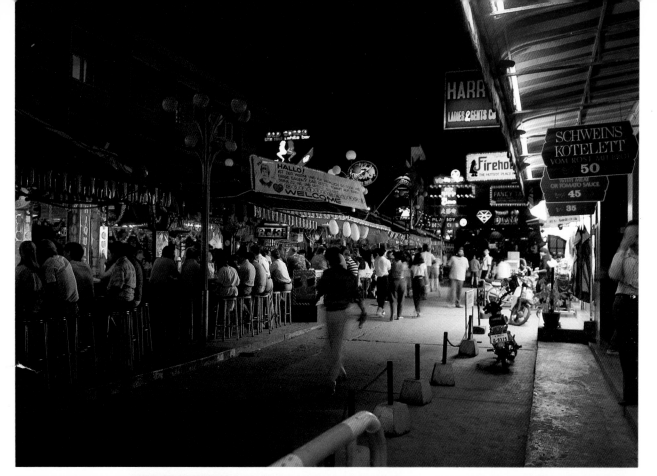

CONTENTS